Ronald

gothetis, Paul,

stiano Ronaldo : [international

ccer star] /

.07

3 4028 096

S0-ADK-693

HARRIS COUNTY PUBLIC LIBRARY

WITHDRAWN

CRISTIANO RONALDO

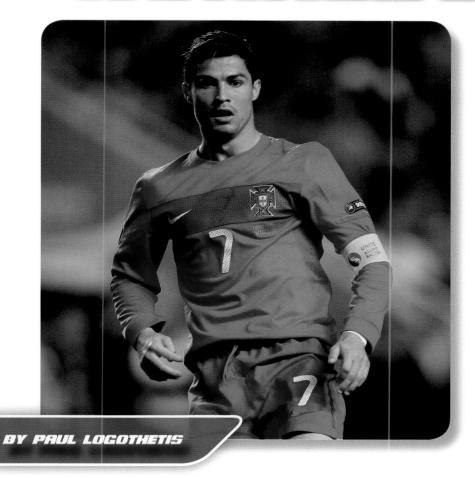

BY PAUL LOGOTHETIS

SportsZone

An Imprint of Abdo Publishing
abdopublishing.com

abdopublishing.com

Published by Abdo Publishing, a division of ABDO, PO Box 398166, Minneapolis, Minnesota 55439. Copyright © 2016 by Abdo Consulting Group, Inc. International copyrights reserved in all countries. No part of this book may be reproduced in any form without written permission from the publisher. SportsZone™ is a trademark and logo of Abdo Publishing.

Printed in the United States of America, North Mankato, Minnesota
042015
092015

 THIS BOOK CONTAINS
RECYCLED MATERIALS

Cover Photo: Mike Egerton/Press Association/AP Images
Interior Photos: Mike Egerton/Press Association/AP Images, 1; Francisco Seco/AP Images, 4; Manu Fernandez/AP Images, 7, 17, 29; Paulo Duarte/AP Images, 8, 11, 12; Sergey Ponomarev/AP Images, 15; Claude Paris/AP Images, 18; Andres Kudacki/AP Images, 21, 23; Daniel Ochoa de Olza/AP Images, 24; Kieran McManus/Rex Features/AP Images, 27;

Editor: Nick Rebman
Series Designer: Craig Hinton

Library of Congress Control Number: 2015931750

Cataloging-in-Publication Data

Logothetis, Paul.
 Cristiano Ronaldo: International soccer star / Paul Logothetis.
   p. cm. -- (Playmakers)
Includes bibliographical references and index.
ISBN 978-1-62403-841-9
1. Ronaldo, Cristiano, 1985- --Juvenile literature. 2. Soccer players--Portugal--Biography--Juvenile literature.   I. Title.
796.334092--dc23
[B]   2015931750

TABLE OF CONTENTS

Cristiano Ronaldo

CHAPTER 1

A YOUNG STAR

Cristiano Ronaldo received the pass. He sprinted forward with an open field in front of him. Only Sweden's keeper stood in his way. Ronaldo fired a shot. The ball landed in the back of the net. Ronaldo's teammates jumped on him to celebrate. It was his third goal of the night for Portugal.

Portugal beat Sweden 3–2. Ronaldo had scored all of his team's goals. And the victory meant Portugal

Ronaldo dribbles the ball during Portugal's World Cup qualifying game against Sweden in 2013.

was going to the World Cup. No one doubted that Ronaldo was one of the best players in the world.

Ronaldo has done a lot of work for charities. He has given lots of money to hospitals. He also works with Save the Children. This group fights child hunger and obesity.

Cristiano grew up without much money. His family lived in a small apartment. It was in a poor area of a city called Funchal. The city is on the island of Madeira. And the island is part of Portugal. That is a European country on the Atlantic Ocean.

Cristiano fell in love with soccer at an early age. He played in the narrow streets around his home. After school he did whatever he could to get outside. His mother would ask him whether his homework was done. Cristiano would say he did not have any. His mother knew better. She sent him to his room to do it. But he sometimes climbed out the window. He wanted to play soccer with his friends.

Ronaldo, *left*, competes in a game against Barcelona in 2012.

Cristiano's skill soon became clear. He was very fast and ran right around other players. For that reason, people gave him the nickname "Little Bee."

Madeira has two major clubs on the island. They are called C. D. Nacional and C. S. Marítimo. Cristiano was only 10 years old. But already, both clubs wanted Cristiano to play for them. He agreed to meet with both clubs. Then he would make a decision. But Marítimo did not show up for the meeting. So Cristiano chose Nacional.

Cristiano Ronaldo

CHAPTER 2

LEAVING HOME

Cristiano Ronaldo was stubborn. He wanted to make every play by himself. But he learned how to become a team player at Nacional. He learned that the team had more success when he was not selfish.

Cristiano stood out from the other boys on the team. But Cristiano's parents wanted him to keep improving. They knew he would have to play against better teams. That meant he would have to leave

Ronaldo plays in his first game as a member of Portugal's national team.

Madeira. It was not an easy decision. Cristiano had never been off the island. He had never been away from his family.

Cristiano got on a plane for the first time. He flew to Lisbon. That is the capital of Portugal. He had a tryout with Sporting Lisbon. This team was one of the best in Portugal. Cristiano was very nervous the night before his tryout. He did not sleep. But he believed in his abilities. The next day, he impressed the coaches. They asked him to join the team.

Ronaldo is very popular in his hometown. Pictures of him greet people at the airport. When Ronaldo goes back to Madeira, he always visits his favorite restaurant. And he always orders a plate of fish.

Cristiano played very well at Sporting. He spent hours every day practicing. He also spent time staying in shape. Sometimes he strapped weights to his feet before practicing. That way he would be even faster when he took the weights off.

Many people began to notice Cristiano's speed and skill. Alex Ferguson was one of them. He was the coach of

An 18-year-old Ronaldo, *right*, competes for the ball in a 2003 game as a member of Sporting Lisbon.

Manchester United. That is one of the top teams in England. Manchester United plays in the Premier League. This league has some of the best teams in the world. Ferguson believed Cristiano could be a superstar. He wanted Cristiano on his team. But other teams wanted him, too. So Manchester United acted quickly. The club paid millions to Sporting Lisbon. Now Cristiano was a member of Manchester United. And he looked forward to showing his talent.

Cristiano Ronaldo

CHAPTER 3

MANCHESTER UNITED

Cristiano Ronaldo arrived in Manchester, England, in 2003. Fans were excited about the young player from Portugal. Ronaldo was only 18 years old. So Ferguson decided to ease Ronaldo into the team. That meant Ronaldo began most games on the bench. He usually entered the game in the second half. His speed and skill were the perfect weapon against tired opponents. Ferguson had high hopes for Ronaldo. The coach gave him

Ronaldo dribbles the ball as a member of Manchester United in 2009.

the famous No. 7 jersey. Many of Manchester United's greatest players had worn that number.

Ronaldo was making a lot of money. He told his mother to stop working. His whole family moved to England to be near him. Ronaldo always enjoyed having a house full of friends and family. He felt that life was easier when he could joke and be happy.

Ronaldo is very famous. That makes it hard for him to enjoy a regular life. Some women sent him wedding rings in the mail. They wanted to marry him! But Ronaldo likes to do normal things. He goes out for dinner with friends. He also likes to dance.

After the season ended, it was time for the European Championship. In this tournament, players play for their home country. So Ronaldo played for Portugal. Ronaldo was one of the best young players in the event. He led his team all the way to the final match. But Ronaldo left the field in tears. Greece defeated Portugal 1–0.

Ronaldo, *right*, heads the ball into the goal during the Champions League final in 2008.

Ronaldo's career was taking off. But he was feeling great sadness. His father died in 2005. Ronaldo did not stop playing, though. He dedicated his goals to his father. He was inspired by his father's memory.

In 2007 Ronaldo was named the best player in the Premier League. He helped Manchester United win the championship. But Ronaldo did more than score goals. He also kept the fans entertained. People were amazed by his dribbling skills.

Manchester United was now focused on the Champions League. This tournament is for the best club teams in Europe. Ronaldo led Manchester United to the 2008 final. The game was against Chelsea. Ronaldo scored Manchester United's only goal. Chelsea scored a goal, too. The game ended in a tie. So the winner was decided by a penalty kick shootout. Ronaldo missed his shot. But his teammates made all of their kicks. And Chelsea missed its last shot. Manchester United had won the Champions League title for the first time since 1999.

Wayne Rooney was Ronaldo's teammate at Manchester United. In the 2006 World Cup, Rooney played for England. Ronaldo played for Portugal. And he helped Portugal beat England. Ronaldo returned to Manchester United after the World Cup. He was still good friends with Rooney.

Manchester United won the Premier League again the next season. And the club also got back to the Champions League final. This time it was against Barcelona. Lionel Messi was Barcelona's star player. People said Messi and Ronaldo were

Ronaldo hangs his head after Barcelona scores a goal against Manchester United in the 2009 Champions League final.

the two best players in the world. Manchester United started the game well. Ronaldo nearly scored. But the ball hit the post. Barcelona took control after that. Messi sealed Barcelona's victory. He jumped high and scored on a header. Barcelona won the game 2–0.

It was Ronaldo's last game for Manchester United. It was also the start of a great rivalry with Messi.

Cristiano Ronaldo

CHAPTER 4

REAL MADRID

In 2009 Cristiano Ronaldo left Manchester United. He joined Real Madrid. That is one of the best clubs in Spain. Lionel Messi played for Barcelona. That is another top Spanish club. Now the world's two best players were playing in the same league. Fans could not wait to see them face off.

Real Madrid was not doing well when Ronaldo arrived. The club had not won any trophies in two

Ronaldo runs down the field during his first season with Spanish powerhouse Real Madrid.

seasons. For most clubs, this would be normal. But Real Madrid was used to winning. Two seasons without a trophy seemed like a crisis.

Barcelona was Real Madrid's biggest rival. Some people thought Barcelona was the best team ever. Ronaldo hoped to change that. He scored 26 league goals. He did it in 29 games. But it was not enough. Real Madrid could not get past Barcelona and Messi. Barcelona won the league title. And Messi led the league with 34 goals.

In the 2011–12 season, Ronaldo scored against every team in the Spanish league. He was the first player to do that. He was also the first player to score in six straight *Clásicos*. The *Clásico* is the match between Real Madrid and Barcelona.

Ronaldo and Messi continued their rivalry. They chased each other for trophies and goals. Ronaldo scored 40 goals in the 2010–11 season. Messi scored 31. The next season Ronaldo scored 46 goals. But Messi did even better. Messi set a record with 50.

Messi, *left*, tries to get the ball away from Ronaldo at a 2011 game in Barcelona.

In 2011 Real Madrid played Barcelona in the King's Cup final. The King's Cup is a tournament for Spanish teams of all professional levels. The game against Barcelona went to overtime. Ronaldo leaped high to head home the winner. Then he slid into the corner to celebrate. Ronaldo and his team were relieved. They had finally gotten past their rivals. It was Ronaldo's first trophy with his new club.

Ronaldo was the star of the team. His talent was clear for all to see. He scored on 30-yard free kicks. The ball would take off over the defensive wall. It would swivel through the air. It would zoom past the leaping keeper. Ronaldo would also jump high to head home some of his goals.

Ronaldo helps sick people when he can. For example, a baby in Spain needed surgery. Ronaldo was asked to donate a jersey and some shoes. People thought it would help raise money. Instead, Ronaldo paid for the whole operation. It cost more than $75,000.

Real Madrid won the Spanish league in 2012–13. It was the club's first league title in four years. But the trophy felt a little empty. Real Madrid did not win the Champions League. The club missed the final game for the third straight year.

Ronaldo holds up the King's Cup trophy after defeating Barcelona in 2011.

CHAPTER 5

EUROPEAN SUCCESS

Real Madrid hired a new coach in 2013. Carlo Ancelotti had lots of experience. In Italy, he had won the Champions League as a player. He had also won it as a coach. Now he wanted to lead Real Madrid to the title. He said his team had to be more aggressive. This was perfect for Cristiano Ronaldo.

But Ronaldo was not the only star on the team. Real Madrid was loaded with *galácticos*. That is a

Real Madrid coach Carlo Ancelotti, *right*, speaks to Ronaldo during a game in 2014.

word for famous players who are paid a lot of money. All of Real Madrid's *galácticos* wanted to play. The coach managed them well. One thing did not change, though. Ronaldo still played almost every game from start to finish.

In 2015 Ronaldo won his third Golden Ball trophy. The trophy is given to the world's best player. Ronaldo first won it in 2008. But then Messi won four in a row. Only 10 players have won the award more than once.

In Europe, soccer clubs play for several trophies each year. They play for the league title. That trophy is for the team with the best record in the league. They play for the league cup. That trophy is for the winner of a tournament. The best teams also play for the Champions League title. That trophy is the most important prize for teams in Europe.

Real Madrid usually has a good chance at winning the league and cup titles. But those trophies are not enough for this proud club. Real Madrid has always been focused on winning the Champions League.

Ronaldo prepares to take a shot against Borussia Dortmund in a 2014 Champions League game.

The 2013–14 season was starting. Real Madrid's fans were impatient. It had been 12 years since the club's last Champions League title. Ronaldo wanted to lead his team to glory. He scored three goals in the first Champions League game. In fact, he scored nine goals in six matches. In another game, he scored four times. This helped Real Madrid reach the quarterfinals. There they played Borussia Dortmund. That team had eliminated Real Madrid the year before. The crowd roared as Ronaldo scored in Real Madrid's 3–0 win.

Ronaldo has had a lot of success with Portugal's national team. He is the country's all-time leading scorer. But it was not enough in the 2014 World Cup. Portugal did not do well in the tournament.

Real Madrid made it all the way to the final. There they faced Atlético Madrid. The teams were from the same city. It was the first time that happened in the final. The game took place in Ronaldo's home country of Portugal. So the game was even more special for him. Atlético had won the Spanish title only days before. And Real Madrid had won the King's Cup again. The winner of this game would finish the season with two trophies.

Atlético scored first. Time was winding down. It looked like the game would end 1–0. But Real Madrid scored in the last minute. The game was tied 1–1. It went into extra time. That was when Ronaldo and his teammates took charge.

Ronaldo lifts the Champions League trophy after defeating Atlético Madrid in 2014.

Real Madrid scored three more goals. Ronaldo scored one of them on a penalty kick. Real Madrid won the game 4–1. Finally, the club had won another Champions League title. Ronaldo and the team returned to Madrid the next day. They had a huge celebration.

Ronaldo has won almost every trophy possible with Real Madrid and Manchester United. People will remember him as one of soccer's greatest players.

FUN FACTS AND QUOTES

- Ronaldo's mother named her son after Ronald Reagan. Reagan was the US president from 1981 to 1989. Ronaldo's mother felt the name was very strong.

- Ronaldo has always had a bad temper. He was sent home from school one day after throwing a chair at a teacher. As a boy, he would cry if a teammate lost the ball. He earned the nickname "Crybaby."

- Ronaldo enjoys singing. He even sang a song as part of a commercial for one of his sponsors in Portugal.

- *"He is easily the best player in the world. He is better than Kaka and better than Messi. . . . His contribution as a goal threat is unbelievable. His stats are incredible. Strikes at goal, attempts on goal, raids into the penalty box, headers. It is all there. Absolutely astounding."* —Alex Ferguson talking about Ronaldo in 2009

- Ronaldo has his own museum on his home island of Madeira. He also has his own line of underwear and shirts. He even has his own app for smartphones.

- Portugal has produced some of soccer's best players. They include Eusébio, Luís Figo, and Rui Costa. But many people consider Ronaldo to be the best Portuguese player of all time.

WEBSITES

To learn more about Playmakers, visit **booklinks.abdopublishing.com**. These links are routinely monitored and updated to provide the most current information available.

GLOSSARY

assist
A pass to a teammate that leads to a goal.

defender
A player whose position is in front of the keeper to help stop opponents from scoring.

dribble
A move that allows a player to control the ball and move it upfield.

galácticos
A Spanish word for famous players who are paid a lot of money. Real Madrid has spent lots of money to get many of the world's best players.

header
Using one's head to guide the ball.

keeper
The player who defends the goal and can use his hands.

midfielder
A player whose position is between the defenders and strikers.

striker
The team's best scorer, who plays more forward than everyone else.

substitute
A player who comes off the bench to replace another on the field.

INDEX

FURTHER RESOURCES

Jökulsson, Illugi. *Ronaldo*. New York: Abbeville Kids, 2014.

Part, Michael. *Cristiano Ronaldo: The Rise of a Winner*. Los Angeles: Sole Books, 2014.

Torres, John Albert. *Soccer Star Cristiano Ronaldo*. Berkeley Heights, NJ: Speeding Star, 2014.